VOLUME TWO

Conversations with the Eucharistic Heart of Jesus

Direction for Our Times
As given to Anne,
a lay apostle

VOLUME TWO

Direction for Our Times
As given to Anne, a lay apostle

ISBN: 978-0-9766841-1-4

Library of Congress Number: applied for

Publisher: Direction for Our Times

In Ireland:
Direction for Our Times
The Hague Building
Cullies
Cavan
Co. Cavan
Ireland
+353-(0)49-437-3040

In the USA:
Direction for Our Times
9000 West 81st Street
Justice, IL 60458
USA

708-496-9300

www.directionforourtimes.org

How to Pray the Rosary information, is used with permission. Copyright © Congregation of Marians of the Immaculate Conception, Stockbridge, MA 01263. www.marian.org.

Paintings of *Jesus Christ the Returning King* and *Our Lady Queen of the Church* by Janusz Antosz

V1014

DIOCESE OF KILMORE

Tel: 049 4331496
Fax: 049 4361796
Email: bishop@kilmorediocese.ie
Website: www.kilmorediocese.ie

Bishop's House
Cullies
Cavan
Co. Cavan

To Whom It May Concern:

Direction For Our Times (DFOT) is a religious movement founded by "Anne", a lay apostle from our diocese, who wishes to remain anonymous. The movement is in its infancy and does not as yet enjoy canonical status. I have asked a priest of the diocese, Fr.Connolly, to assist in the work of the movement and to ensure that in all its works and publications it remains firmly within the teaching and practice of the Catholic Church.

I have known "Anne", the founder of the movement, for several years. She is a Catholic in good standing in the diocese, a wife and mother of small children, and a woman of deep spirituality. From the beginning she has always been anxious that everything connected with the movement be subject to the authority of the Church. She has submitted all her writings to me and will not publish anything without my permission. She has submitted her writings to the Congregation of the Doctrine of the Faith and I have done so as well.

In so far as I am able to judge she is orthodox in her writings and teachings. Her spirituality and the spiritual path that she proposes to those who wish to accept it are in conformity with the teachings of the Church and of the great spiritual writers of the past and present.

Leo O'Reilly.

Date _16 June '06_

+Leo O'Reilly
Bishop of Kilmore

Diocesan Seal

DIOCESE OF KILMORE

Tel: 049-4331496
Fax: 049-4361796
Email: bishop@kilmorediocese.ie
Website: www.kilmorediocese.ie

Bishop's House
Cullies
Cavan
Co. Cavan

2 September 2011

To Whom It May Concern:

I offer an update on the present status of Anne, a lay apostle and Direction for Our Times.

I initially granted permission for the distribution of the messages and written materials of Anne. This position remains unchanged. The writings and materials may continue to be distributed. As pointed out in my letter on the DFOT website, the permission to distribute the messages does not imply a final judgment on whether they are authentic private revelation. A final judgment on that question must await the outcome of an official Church inquiry into these matters.

Following Church protocol, I set up a diocesan commission over a year ago to inquire into the writings of Anne and to evaluate her reports of receiving messages from heaven. That work of evaluation is continuing and the outcome of it will be made public in due course.

I hope this statement is helpful in the clarification of these matters.

Yours sincerely in Christ,

Leo O'Reilly
Bishop of Kilmore.

October 11, 2004

Dear Friends,

I am very much impressed with the messages delivered by Anne who states that they are received from God the Father, Jesus, and the Blessed Mother. They provide material for excellent and substantial meditation for those to whom they are intended, namely to the laity, to bishops and priests; and sinners with particular difficulties. These messages should not be read hurriedly but reserved for a time when heartfelt recollection and examination can be made.

I am impressed by the complete dedication of Anne to the authority of the magisterium, to her local Bishop and especially to the Holy Father. She is a very loyal daughter of the Church.

Sincerely in Christ,

Philip M. Hannan

Archbishop Philip M. Hannan, (Ret.)
President of FOCUS Worldwide Network
Retired Archbishop of New Orleans

PMH/aac

Dr. Mark I. Miravalle, S.T.D.

Professor of Theology and Mariology, Franciscan University of Steubenville
313 High Street • Hopedale, OH 43976 • U.S.A.
740-937-2277 • mmiravalle@franciscan.edu

Without in any way seeking to anticipate the final and definitive judgment of the local bishop and of the Holy See (to which we owe our filial obedience of mind and heart), I wish to manifest my personal discernment concerning the nature of the messages received by "Anne," a Lay Apostle.

After an examination of the reported messages and an interview with the visionary herself, I personally believe that the messages received by "Anne" are of supernatural origin.

The message contents are in conformity with the faith and morals teachings of the Catholic Church's Magisterium and in no way violate orthodox Catholic doctrine. The phenomena of the precise manner of how the messages are transmitted (i.e., the locutions and visions) are consistent with the Church's historical precedence for authentic private revelation. The spiritual fruits (cf. Mt. 7:17-20) of Christian faith, conversion, love, and interior peace, based particularly upon a renewed awareness of the indwelling Christ and prayer before the Blessed Sacrament, have been significantly manifested in various parts of the world within a relatively brief time since the messages have been received and promulgated. Hence the principal criteria used by ecclesiastical commissions to investigate reported supernatural events (message, phenomena, and spiritual fruits) are, in my opinion, substantially satisfied in the case of "Anne's" experience.

The messages which speak of the coming of Jesus Christ, the "Returning King" do not refer to an imminent end of the world with Christ's final physical coming, but rather call for a spiritual receptivity to an ongoing spiritual return of Jesus Christ, a dynamic advent of Jesus which ushers in a time of extraordinary grace and peace for humanity (in ways similar to the Fatima promise for an eventual era of peace as a result of the Triumph of the Immaculate Heart of Mary, or perhaps the "new springtime" for the Church referred to by the words of the great John Paul II).

As "Anne" has received permission from her local ordinary, Bishop Leo O'Reilly, for the spreading of her messages, and has also submitted all her writings to the Congregation for the Doctrine of the Faith, I would personally encourage, (as the Church herself permits), the prayerful reading of these messages, as they have constituted an authentic spiritual benefit for a significant number of Catholic leaders throughout the world.

Mark Miravalle

Dr. Mark Miravalle
Professor of Theology and Mariology
Franciscan University of Steubenville
October 13, 2006

Table of Contents

Introduction

Dear Reader,

I am a wife, mother of six, and a Secular Franciscan.

At the age of twenty, I was divorced for serious reasons and with pastoral support in this decision. In my mid-twenties I was a single parent, working and bringing up a daughter. As a daily Mass communicant, I saw my faith as sustaining and had begun a journey toward unity with Jesus, through the Secular Franciscan Order or Third Order.

My sister travelled to Medjugorje and came home on fire with the Holy Spirit. After hearing of her beautiful pilgrimage, I experienced an even more profound conversion. During the following year I experienced various levels of deepened prayer, including a dream of the Blessed Mother, where she asked me if I would work for Christ. During the dream she showed me that this special spiritual work would mean I would be separated from others in the world. She actually showed me my extended family and how I would be separated from them. I told her that I did not care. I would do anything asked of me.

Shortly after, I became sick with endometriosis. I have been sick ever since, with one thing or another. My sicknesses are always the types that mystify doctors in the beginning. This is part of the cross and I mention it because so many suffer in this way. I was told by my doctor that I would never conceive children. As a single parent, this did not concern me as I assumed it was God's will. Soon after, I met a wonderful man. My first marriage had been annulled and we married and conceived five children.

Spiritually speaking, I had many experiences that included what I now know to be interior locutions. These moments were beautiful and the words still stand out firmly in my heart, but I did not get excited because I was busy offering up illnesses and exhaustion. I took it as a matter of course that Jesus had to work hard to sustain me as He had given me a lot to handle. In looking back, I see that He was preparing me to do His work. My preparation period was long, difficult and not very exciting. From the outside, I think people thought, 'That woman has bad luck.' From the inside, I saw that while my sufferings were painful and long lasting, my little family was growing in love, in size and in wisdom, in the sense that my husband and I certainly understood what was important and what was not important. Our continued crosses did that for us.

Various circumstances compelled my husband and me to move with our children far from my loved ones. I offered this up and must say it is the most difficult thing I have had to contend with. Living in exile brings many beautiful opportunities to align with Christ's will; however, you have to continually remind yourself that you are doing that. Otherwise you just feel sad. After several years in exile, I finally got the inspiration to go to Medjugorje. It was actually a gift from my husband for my fortieth birthday. I had tried to go once before, but circumstances prevented the trip and I understood it was not God's will. Finally, though, it was time and my eldest daughter and I found ourselves in front of St. James Church. It was her second trip to Medjugorje.

I did not expect or consider that I would experience anything out of the ordinary. At any rate, we had a beautiful five days. I experienced a spiritual healing on the mountain. My daughter rested and prayed. A quiet but significant thing happened to me. During my Communions, I spoke with Jesus conversationally. I thought this was beautiful, but it had happened before on occasion so I was not stunned or overcome. I remember telling others that Communions in Medjugorje were powerful. I came home, deeply grateful to Our Lady for bringing us there.

The conversations continued all that winter. At some time in the six months that followed our trip, the conversations leaked into my life and came at odd times throughout the day. Jesus began to direct me with decision and I found it more and more difficult to refuse when He asked me to do this or that. I told no one.

During this time, I also began to experience direction from the Blessed Mother. Their voices are not hard to distinguish. I do not hear them in an auditory way, but in my soul or mind. By this time I knew that something remarkable was occurring and Jesus was telling me that He had special work for me, over and above my primary vocation as wife and mother. He told me to write the messages down and that He would arrange to have them published and disseminated. Looking back, it took Him a long time to get me comfortable enough where I was willing to trust Him. I trust His voice now and will continue to do my best to serve Him, given my constant struggle with weaknesses, faults, and the pull of the world.

Please pray for me as I continue to try to serve Jesus. Please answer "yes" to Him because He so badly needs us and He is so kind. He will take you right into His heart if you let Him. I am praying for you and am so grateful to God that He has given you these words. Anyone who knows Him must fall in love with Him, such is His goodness. If you have been struggling, this is your answer. He is coming to you in a special way through these words and the graces that flow through them.

Please do not fall into the trap of thinking that He cannot possibly mean for you to reach high levels of holiness. As I say somewhere in my writings, the greatest sign of the times is Jesus having to make do with the likes of me as His secretary. I consider myself the B-team, dear friends. Join me and together we will do our little bit for Him.

Message received from Jesus immediately following my writing of the above biographical information:

You see, My child, that you and I have been together for a long time. I was working quietly in your life for years before you began this work. Anne, how I love you. You can look back through your life and see so many "yes" answers to Me. Does that not please you and make you glad? You began to say "yes" to Me long before you experienced extraordinary graces. If you had not, My dearest, I could never have given you the graces or assigned this mission to you. Do you see how important it was that you got up every day, in your ordinary life, and said "yes" to your God, despite difficulty, temptation, and hardship? You could not see the big plan as I saw it. You had to rely on your faith. Anne, I tell you today, it is still that way. You cannot see My plan, which is bigger than your human mind can accept. Please continue to rely on your faith as it brings Me such glory. Look at how much I have been able to do with you, simply because you made a quiet and humble decision for Me. Make another quiet and humble decision on this day and every day, saying, "I will serve God." Last night you served Me by bringing comfort to a soul in pain. You decided against yourself and for Me, through your service to him. There was gladness in heaven, Anne. You are Mine. I am yours. Stay with Me, My child. Stay with Me.

The Allegiance Prayer
For All Lay Apostles

Dear God in Heaven, I pledge my allegiance to You. I give You my life, my work and my heart. In turn, give me the grace of obeying Your every direction to the fullest possible extent. Amen.

August 17, 2003
Jesus

My children, I am speaking to you from the depth of My Eucharistic heart. My dearest little souls of this world, you must come back to Me. I want your love now, as never before, and I want to protect you as never before. Because our time is not like your time, I can communicate with you in a timeless manner. This is what I wish to tell you. I am going to share My deepest secrets with you. I am going to remove the veil from the tabernacle as never before. I want you to know Me. I want you to know Me in My miraculous form of the Consecrated Host. I am the Bread of Life. Yes. And I am your Jesus, also. I was a humble man, who walked your paths of difficulty, want, and hardship. Many treated Me badly, so I understand the pain of hurt. We had little money, so I understand the pain of hunger. I was different, so I understand the pain of isolation. Little ones, I am with you. I want to teach you things that souls of past times did not learn until they came to Heaven. I am doing this because I am raising up a tidal wave of Christians to wash over the shore of badness that has taken control of this world, so lovingly created by My Father. This process will cleanse your

1

world, making it safe once again for God's children. I am going to bring you knowledge, wisdom, and love. I am going to introduce you to the divine to make your hearts burn like furnaces of divine love. You will be given the opportunity to work with Me. Children, come with Me now. Walk this walk of the divine with Me, your Savior. Together, we call out to others to join us. In this way, we rise up against evil and reclaim goodness for the world, for its people, and for God in Heaven. I am omnipotent. By cooperating with Me and working with Me, you share in My power. You will learn to love in a way you have never known before. I am revealing Myself in a new way, such as I have never done. Come, let us together pay homage and pledge obedience to God the Father. It is He who decrees this work. Thank Him often and deeply for these graces, for with these graces, you will help Me to save the world.

August 18, 2003
Jesus

I want to show My children the great devotion I have for them. I reside in tabernacles all over the world. I do this because I desire My children to have a living Christ in their midst. Such holiness is available to souls who visit and venerate Me in the Eucharist. I am the cure for every ill. I am the calm for every storm. I am the comfort for every sorrow. Because I intend to lead My children in a more enhanced way, I am going to show you the Life that is enclosed in each tabernacle. My dear ones, if you but knew the value of each and every visit that is made to Me here, there would be crowds all through every day and every night. It is this crowd of souls I invite now. Dear children of this world, I, your Jesus, am not limited by the laws of nature. I can do anything. My powers are unimaginable to souls who have not seen the heavenly vision. In other words, to souls who remain on earth. Much is said in your world about power. This one has this power and that one has another power. Children are being deluged with images of occult or magical powers. I want this to cease. There is an obsession with powers that are NOT heavenly powers. My children, even some

3

of My children of light, say these are good things, or at least harmless. I tell you now, in all of My Godly Majesty, that if a power is not from Me, it is evil. Search every day for these impostors and remove them from your life. You do not see the damage being done, but I, your Savior, assure you that this opens a door to your soul that you do not want opened. Your children must be protected from entertainment or games that feature "powers."

I wish to guide you in this specific manner. I wish to warn and correct you. I wish to teach you. Most of all, I wish to love you. Have you ever loved someone passionately, but been rejected? Was your love ever tossed casually back at you? If this has ever happened to you, then you understand how I feel. I am rejected by the majority of humanity. I gave My very life for this humanity, so that their sins would be overlooked and forgotten. Humanity, poor foolish humanity, flings this gift back at My feet, as if to say, "Your gift is worthless. It has no value anymore." Dearest children, this is ignorance in some cases. Many of these children do not understand that the gift they toss aside is their eternity, their salvation. They do not understand this in many cases because they are not being told. I will rectify this situation shortly when I reveal Myself to your world, leaving no room for doubt that Jesus Christ lives and that Jesus Christ saves. At that time, souls will know Me and will be free to make a choice based on knowledge. My little one, how consoled I will be by the souls who make the choice in advance of that day, based on faith. I am sending My Spirit into the world now. The Spirit, the third person of the Trinity, is resting upon every soul who welcomes Him. My words must be spread and when these words reach a soul who is housing the Spirit, that soul will light up in a spectacular manner. Truly, the light of each of these souls will reach Heaven, where the triumphant ones will rejoice to see another soldier returning to the cause. Be alert, dear ones, to My every whim. Practice responding in obedience to My requests. You will walk in peace, I promise you that today. Adore Me in the Eucharist as I teach you about love.

August 19, 2003
Jesus

I wish to speak to you today about love. I am all love. All love is Me. My children of this world must learn about love again, because, for many, the essence of love has been so distorted, they do not recognize it as valuable or seek to obtain it. Love is quiet and steady, My children. Love can be relied upon. Love does not diminish in the face of temptation. There are many kinds of love upon earth and all genuine love has its place. I want My children to examine the genuine opportunities for love in their lives. Certainly a family is a primary source of love. But many families have failed in love and their members drift away in bitterness. Children, the obligation to love someone does not mean you will not be hurt. On the contrary, often, and I must say usually, this obligation to love insures that you will be hurt and it carries with it another obligation and that is the obligation to forgive. If you would like to see an example of someone who has been hurt, look at Me. You did not deserve to be hurt, little one. I understand and I see everything. I also did not deserve to be hurt. I tell you now, dearest ones, that you have hurt Me many times. Your neglect alone wounds Me terribly. But I love you. I understand you are not perfect. I look upon you and, truly, I forgive you. Please accept My forgiveness and let us begin our walk together anew. Please, dear wounded child, take My forgiveness into your heart and let it make a home there. If a guest is welcome, a guest causes little trouble to his host because a guest who feels truly welcome will make himself at home and not cause his host any trouble. A welcome guest sees to his own needs and seeks to help his host. Isn't that true, dear one? I am your Guest. I am a Guest in your soul. Make Me welcome and I will heal, nourish, and recover your soul. Your heart will beat only with love. I will cleanse the bitterness and permanently remove the hurt. I will leave such a surplus of forgiveness that you will have plenty to lavish upon those who have hurt you. Dear children of this one true God, seek out people who have hurt you, especially in your family, and offer your forgiveness. You don't need to look for it. Ask Me where it is, dear child, and indeed, I will hand forgiveness to you. If you do this, you will heal. You may say, "Jesus, it is too hard. I cannot do this as I have been hurt too badly." My child, again I counsel you to practice. Say these words of forgiveness in your head. Then say them aloud. Become used to the sound of them. With My graces, it will not only be possible, it will be easy. Trust Me, who loves you with a genuine love and seeks your peace. I want no barrier of bitterness between us. I want to heal you. I want to heal families. Do not be afraid. If someone rejects your forgiveness, that is his loss. You will heal, and you will be rewarded. It matters not to Me what a recipient does with a gift you have given. I look only at the fact that you have given when I examine your life. So welcome Me as your Guest, My beloved one. I will put so much love and forgiveness in your heart that you will not be able to give it away fast enough. I am your God. Believe in Me.

August 20, 2003
Jesus

Today I speak to you about unity. There is great disunity in the world. This disunity has permeated most modern life, but I speak in a particular way of disunity within the family. I intend to return a sense of unity to every family that will allow Me to do so. My children, when there is family unity, the members experience a steady flow of love. My peace, always available, draws the family through the inevitable times of difficulty and members of such families possess a calm and steady bearing. Prayer will bring unity to a family in a swift manner. If a family makes a decision to make family prayer a priority, I can bestow many graces to that home. Families devoted to our Mother already understand this connection between prayer and family unity. I want this for all families. Make a firm decision on when your family will pray together. If something interferes with this time, do not take that as a sign that your prayer commitment was a mistake. Simply reschedule to a more suitable time. I, your Jesus, am watching. I understand all. If you tell Me that your family never has enough time together to pray, I will help you to find that time. It is possible you are all too busy and should eliminate certain activities. My children of this busy world must understand the very significant difference between entertainment and duty. An obligation to meet with friends is not as important as an obligation to family prayer, and it is possible that your priorities require examination. Do not fear this examination because I will help you. Together, we will examine your life and see where we can schedule time for you to draw your family together in prayer. Believe Me when I tell you that you will be abundantly blessed in this decision. I will put unity in your family.

Unity is also important for the purpose of identity. Children, in particular, must understand that they are expected to view life and respond to life differently because they are Christians. This begins in your home. My youngest children of this world do not understand their inheritance. With many of My adult children, it is more serious. They have rejected their inheritance. So our goal is twofold. We must educate our youth and call out in love to our adults. Look at your brothers and sisters in the world. Many are experiencing disunity in their families and walk in bitterness. They do not appeal to Me for help. They simply accept that this is how people behave. I assure you, My children, Christians do not behave this way. I intend to bring families together. From this secure love source, children will learn responsibility to others and to God. I intend for this to be the norm again. Will you help Me? Let us agree today that each family will respond to this message by praying together. Start small, if you must, with one Our Father. Then advance gradually. I would like families to pray the Holy Rosary. Let that be your goal. Devotion to My Mother will advance a family to Me very quickly. Devotion to My Mother will heal many deep wounds. My Mother is united with Me in this work and brings many, many souls back to Me. Pray now, as a family, and rejoice as I restore unity to your home.

August 21, 2003
Jesus

Today I wish to direct attention, once again, to the hectic pace of this modern world. Children, come and sit with Me in the Sacrament of the Eucharist. I am in every tabernacle throughout the world. Think of one now, and picture Me there. Do I have a television? A radio? Of course not. Yet I am truly there. "What does He do?" you might ask. I tell you, My child, I am not bored. I think about you. I worry if you are far away. I suffer if you have chosen worldly paths and you are endangering your soul. I am sad each day if there is no hope of a visit from you. I ask My Father to have mercy on you. I direct My angels to watch over you in the hope that someday you will return to Me. My child, how often during your day do you think of Me? You are thinking of Me now, as you read these words. So while your mind is resting upon Me, let Me tell you that I love you. I want only your happiness. I can help you in everything. I can solve your problems and heal your wounds. My child, come and sit before the Eucharist in any tabernacle. My graces and blessings will flow out to you. I want you to sit and soak in the silence. You may close your eyes there and I will fill your precious head with a stream of heavenly thoughts. I have so much to share with you. I have seen every injury you have experienced. I longed to comfort you. Let Me comfort you now.

Again I entreat you to eliminate as much noise from your life as possible. Noise is not conducive to holiness and while you might have to tolerate noise in the world, you can diminish noise in your home and in your car. In silence comes peace, little ones. You will find Me in silence. I am waiting for you and I have never once turned My gaze away from you. You must know that I forgive you for everything. I want only your love.

Souls find this concept difficult because your modern world has scoffed so often at selfless love that souls are suspicious. Why does Jesus love me? I am not very lovable, they think. Indeed, many souls in this world do not like even themselves. So they find it hard to imagine that anyone, particularly the God of All, could desire their well-being and love them completely. I tell you, dear child, that the truth cannot be denied. I am the Truth. And I love you beyond anything you can imagine. My only wish is to bring you back to Me, where I might protect you. Do not be *afraid. You will not be punished for your misdeeds. Come back to Me now and I will pardon your sins. We will proceed together as though these sins had never been committed. Sins leave a certain residue on a soul. Come to Me now, My beloved child, and with a heavenly breath, I will blow away the residue of sin so your soul proceeds in joy and newness.* I am your God. I love you. That will never change.*

---

* See Volume Three, August 9, 2003, regarding the Sacrament of Reconciliation.

August 22, 2003
Jesus

The love in My heart gushes forth upon your world. In an unparalleled manner, I lavish graces on souls. My children, My love is such that I can no longer contain it. I see so many in need of Me, and truly, they shall have Me. Bring My words to those who suffer. My words will be the balm you will use to nurse souls back to wellness. Like heavenly nurses, you will apply My words to every wound and you will see miraculous results. My children, I am working through you. I am using you as healing instruments. Your world is sick and suffers from a disease far worse than any disease of the body. The very soul of your world struggles to find the source of healing it requires. And I am here. I intend to heal your world. I want you to be joyful representatives of your Eucharistic Jesus. The Eucharistic Jesus calls out to His children in firmness. I call you each by name and I say to you, "It is time to return to Me." Come to Me, waiting in the tabernacle, and I will reveal Myself to you in such a way that you will have no doubts. You will be glad in your heart and peaceful in your soul. Rest near the Eucharistic Heart of your Savior and you will be granted everything you need. Faith is a gift, My dear one. I wish to give this gift to you. But you must turn to Me so that I may. My heart beats only with love for you. I can promise you that I will not reproach you. I will help you understand that only joy and light is suitable for a child of God. You will return to us one day. Let us make that the most joyful day of your life. Come to Me, My child, and I will show you how. You say, "Jesus, I forget how to pray." My child, does a small one forget how to cry when he is hurt? Of course not. Come before Me and cry out your pain, your hurt, and your fear. We need not do it all in one day, but take the first step to Me by coming in front of Me. Put yourself in My Eucharistic Presence and I will do the rest. The work will come from Me. I will move you back swiftly to that place that has been reserved for only you in My Sacred Heart. You see, My child, if you have been away from Me, that place has been empty. I, your Jesus, have felt the emptiness terribly as I waited for your return. My heart aches waiting for you, so do not let Me suffer another moment. Do you begin to understand? I love you totally. You were meant to be with Me. Do not let anything hinder your return. I am your God, the God of All. The world wants to trick you out of your inheritance, but I hold it for you. It is safe with Me, My child, so return to Me now, that I may begin to heal you.

August 25, 2003
Jesus

Our work continues. I remain a prisoner in this tabernacle. I wait for every soul who is absent from Me. My children must understand that I am drawing souls to Myself. I can no longer stand by and watch so many souls lost for eternity. In days past, there would be a small number of souls who chose to remain parted from Me for eternity. This caused Me suffering, it is true. In these times, though, My presence in the world and dominion over this world is treated so casually that many souls choosing darkness are led to believe this is almost a meaningless decision. They do not understand the impact. Indeed, some of My children are casual about their eternity because they believe they will have several attempts at life in this world. I tell you today, children, this is a Godless notion created and perpetuated by the evil one who would like to downplay the importance of what you do with this time. There is only one life allotted to each soul. There can be no question about that. Do not believe that you will come back to earth again for another chance. It is this life you are living that will determine your eternity. So, My children, now that we all understand the importance of this day, and this series of days allotted to you, let us make a decision on how you will spend the remainder of your time. I would like you to help Me. I know exactly how many days are left before you appear before Me in the next life. I have special work that needs to be done. Indeed, I have special work for each one of these days remaining to you. If you will say "yes" to Me, I can rest more easily, knowing those tasks will be completed and souls, the certain number attached to your work, will be saved. Additionally, I will have the joy, the happiness of knowing that My immeasurable love for you is returned. My child, come to Me and do My work. You will find no greater joy on this earth. Ask My true followers. They know the ecstasy of feeling My smile in their soul. I want that for you. Let Me assure you that, in most cases, My work for you involves you remaining in your current role. I simply want you to be at peace. I want you to know you are loved. I want to be with you as you struggle and I want to keep you safe. You will experience your days differently when you unite them to Me. What formerly caused distress for you will be barely a ripple against the great peace I am offering. I can take even the smallest, humblest acts of love and obedience and use them to rescue a soul. So instead of merely surviving your time here, you will be using your days, already and always finite, to rescue souls who are living without Me and, in some cases, living against Me. We must have hope for every soul, My dear one. Rest in My tremendous grace during this time as I continue to reveal My great secrets to you.

August 26, 2003
Jesus

Children, I want to speak with you about obedience. I, as your God, am obedient to you. I protect you when I am asked. I render assistance when I am prevailed upon. I created a beautiful world for you to learn about love so you might earn your Heaven. I, your God, am doing My part. I am asking you now to do your part. I speak only from concern, My children. Your world, distorted as it is, seeks to confuse you and make you think that obedience is a negative thing that weakens you. I assure you, My child, I am all-powerful. I am Jesus Christ and if you look at My time in your world, you will see that I was obedient to all whose obedience had call upon Me. I was obedient to God. I was obedient to the laws of that time set forth by the governing rulers. I was obedient to the religious authorities. I was also obedient to My parents. If you study My life you will see a life of holy obedience and meekness. And yet, a man with more power never walked the face of your earth. There is great strength in obedience, and I want to show that to you. Come to Me in the Sacrament of the Eucharist and I will teach you about obedience, revealing its beauty and the strength that lies with this misunderstood virtue. What am I asking of you, you might wonder. I am asking you to obey your Church, first of all. My Church has suffered in this time. Many children have taken this passion time of the Church as a license to be disobedient. Children, this must cease. You are called on to be obedient to your Church and in this way you are obedient to Me. I do not seek your destruction, My child. I seek your salvation. That is why I have given you this Church with all of its wisdom. Many souls say that the world has changed and because of this, the Church must change. Well, I assure you today, I have not changed. Heaven has not changed. You will discover this first-hand one day. The changes have occurred in your world and I am coming to you today through this prophet to tell you that the changes are destroying mankind. Change is not always bad, of course, but your world has deteriorated to an Age of Disobedience and too many souls are being lost. I am intervening in a significant way now to reset the course and direction for you. Heed My words this day. I come to you in love, My children. I bring you unlimited graces. Do not be afraid to change your life, even though it means admitting you have made mistakes. A wise man does not fear mistakes because he knows they are inevitable. Indeed, it is through these mistakes and through the study of past mistakes that we learn for the future. And it is the future I am concerned about. I want your future to be glorious. I want only good things for you. I have the graces necessary to insure that you succeed spiritually. You need not fear that you are not holy enough to follow Me. My child, I know all. I call you because your destiny lies with Me. I am your God and I call you by name into My heavenly service. Do not disappoint Me. Begin by the smallest acts of obedience to your Church and I will lead you to the heights of holiness for which I created you. Fear nothing. Sit with Me in silence and I promise to direct you. You need only come to Me and the changes will begin. How you will welcome these changes. Your world does not offer peace. Peace comes only from Me. Make haste to return to Me for My graces are waiting.

August 27, 2003
Jesus

Today I wish to speak to My children about Heaven. Heaven is real, dear ones. It is a place and I am there. Most of your deceased family members are here along with all of the saints and many others whom you have not met. There is great fellowship in Heaven, particularly among souls who served Me in similar ways. You will feel no pain or fatigue here, but, at times, you will rest in ideas and concepts so that you can learn them. You see, My children, your learning continues and the quenching of the thirst for knowledge is a part of Heaven because everyone is able to learn about any topic that sparks their curiosity. You can then build on that and graduate to even deeper levels of knowledge and knowing. This does not feel like school. It is joy and wonder. It is innocence and love. It is coming into the mystery of your universe in such a way that you then help to direct the universe. My children, because of your limited understanding, which is necessary while you remain on earth, I cannot tell you everything. But I wanted to share this glimpse of Heaven with you and I will continue to part the curtains, as it were, so that you understand where you are going. It is good to know your destination so that you know how to prepare. I, your Jesus, am helping you prepare. If you listen to Me and prepare well, you will be ready for Heaven when it is time to come here. In this way, the day of your earthly death will be the best day of your life. Believe Me, My children, when I tell you that all of us here in Heaven await your coming. We are linked to you. My children on earth like to think that holiness is someone else's call. If you are listening to Me now, you understand that holiness is your call. If your destination is Heaven, and of course it should be, then you must begin your preparation now. You would hardly travel to a foreign country without learning at least something about what you will want and need there. So take heed when I tell you that you will want to practice the virtues while you remain on earth. Try to view it as learning to speak the heavenly language before your arrival here.

I want to tell you, My children, that the saints, everyone here, clamors to assist you now. You are living in dark times and many of you have fallen into a spiritual sleep. I am preparing to make a loud noise, in a manner of speaking, to awaken your world. Better for you, My child, that you open your eyes gently now and begin to serve from love and obedience, as opposed to fear. If you follow Me now, you will nearly eradicate fear from your life. I felt stabs of human fear for fleeting moments, as in the Garden and when I was condemned to death. But My faith and knowledge assured Me that man could hurt My body, but My soul remained intact, belonging to God and this heavenly world. It will be the same for you, children. You will fear nothing. Additionally, if you follow Me, you will receive extraordinary graces to deal with anything that frightens you. I will manage any fears you have, both now and in the future, and this is another solemn promise I make to you. Also, I give you permission to be like small children, often saying to their parents, "You promised!"

August 28, 2003
Jesus

My children, I am with you. You have heard Me say that many times before. Perhaps I have said it so often that you do not really hear it. Today, I want you to both hear these words and understand them. I am with you. Does that mean I watch you from Heaven, hoping all goes well with you? Does it mean I gaze out over My whole world, seeing only the large events? No. I am with you. I am with YOU, My child. That means I see the world from your eyes. I walk your walks and I experience what you experience. I am there when you are hurt. I feel the sting of human unkindness when you experience it. I feel the weakness and pain in your body when you are sick. My compassionate gaze, so filled with love and understanding, rests upon you every minute of every day. I forgive you any sins even before these sins are committed. But you must admit to your sins and ask forgiveness. My child, do not think you have been abandoned. I say with divine solemnity, I am with you.

So, begin to focus on the fact that every minute of every day, your Jesus is present. Talk to Me, dear child. I have so much to tell you. I have the answers for your difficulties. I have explanations for things you do not understand. I have love for people that you do not feel. So if you focus on the reality of My presence, you will begin to rely on Me. My child, then the transition can begin. Once you begin to rely on Me, your life will get easier and less stressful. You will walk away from even the most difficult situations and leave them behind, instead of carrying that worry with you into the next area of your life. You will find this to be so liberating that quite quickly it will become your habit. And then, child, it will be Me working through you. And when that goal is reached, there is no limit to what you can do. Again I say to you today, you must practice for something to become a habit. So today, concentrate on My continual presence. Ask Me what I would like you to do. Ask Me what words I would like you to use. Then listen to My answer. My Spirit will speak to you and you will hear the words, resting upon your soul. In this way, we can communicate all day long. Have faith. I give you faith today, as you take these first steps to unity with Me. There is no situation where you should leave Me. Even in the most difficult of circumstances, call upon Me. Even in sinful conditions, or should I say especially in sinful condi-

tions, cry out to Me. I am there anyway, My child. You cannot hide your sin by ignoring Me and hoping I have gone away. So speak to Me. Say, "Lord, help me." You will not be disappointed. I will help you. I bring you these words today so that you may understand that I am with you. I will never leave you. I await your notice and stand by, ready to assure you that you are cherished by Me and that I did not put you on earth to do work that was too hard for you. If your life is too hard, My little soul, it is because you are trying to accomplish it alone. You need Me. And I am here for you. So let us waste no more time. Jesus, your Jesus, is asking for your attention. Once I have your attention, we can proceed. You will never regret having returned to Me. Do not hesitate. Come and sit before Me in the tabernacle and we will begin.

August 28, 2003
Jesus

I want to draw souls into My Sacred Heart. This is the place of safety for you, My dear ones. It is here, in the security of My love, that you can rest and begin to see your world with clarity. Just as I told you that I see your world through your eyes, because I am always with you, I want you to see all through My eyes. In this way, gradually, you and I become one. When you look at a situation that troubles you, I want you to think, what would My Jesus say about this? If you are unsure, simply ask Me. I will tell you. In the same way, when you look at a situation that causes you joy, ask Me if I also feel joy. We can then exult together. And there is much to be joyful about, My little one. I am joyful, for example, about you. I see your struggles and do you know why seeing your struggles makes Me joyful? Because you are trying to be good. We, in Heaven, observe this struggle for improvement and we send you all manner of little rewards and assistances. We are with you in your struggles, more than you can imagine. My heart beats with such tenderness for you when you struggle. My child, you must not take this struggling as a sign that you are failing, but rather as a sign that you are succeeding. There is little struggle in badness, you see. There is a quiet, ominous acceptance or acquiescence. So do not be afraid. As long as you have the desire to serve Me, I will meet you there, at that initial desire, and I will bring with Me everything you need to succeed. My child, I will make it easy for you. It is not in My nature to confuse, so you must believe that confusion does not come from Me. Fear, anxiety, restlessness do not come from Me. Bitterness, hatred, deceit do not come from Me. Does that mean you will never experience these things? No. It is part of your earthly cross that you will encounter these things. What I am telling you is that you must bring these things to Me. I will then take them from you and you will be free of them. You may encounter these things again, perhaps within the hour. Come back to Me, in your heart, where I remain, and I will take them from you again. You see, My little dear one, your struggles are Mine now. I am stronger, wiser, more able for these things and I want to remove any negative thoughts from you. I seek to heal you and renew you. I can do this if you will let Me. I do not make this promise for now, this moment. I make this a lifetime pledge to you. When you experience a difficulty with your emotions, you bring it right to Me. And that's where it will end. I do not want My children troubled by obsessions. And because you belong to Me, and seek to serve Me, this is a right I bestow upon you. You may think of it as an advance on your eternal inheritance. I intend to give you a portion of the peace we enjoy in Heaven. This is My gift to you and is a special concession for the difficult times you are living. Bring your troubles to Me, little soul of My heart. I, your God, wish to bring you relief.

August 28, 2003
Jesus

On this day I cry out to all families. How My Sacred Heart mourns the loss of so many families. My dear ones, We must work together now to strengthen the Sacrament of Marriage. It is on this sacrament that I base the family. There have always been cases where a family is without one parent. This can sometimes be My will, as when a parent dies. I have My reasons for allowing this to happen. But in most cases, My will involves a man and a woman, united in Holy Matrimony, bringing up children. My dear ones, I have so many reasons for structuring your lives this way that we could speak of nothing else for days. Let Me begin our discussion of families by saying this. I have not changed My will in this matter. Your world would have you believe that both parents are not necessary. Children, this is not the case. A father brings to the family formation that a mother cannot and a mother brings things to a family that do not come from a father. I understand all. As God, I do not require explanations. There are so many cases today where one parent is forced to accept all responsibility. In some cases, this is My will and I do this because I have decided that one parent is damaging to the children. You are responsible for the moral and physical safety of your children and if your children are in an environment where they are unsafe, you have My permission to remove them, either by leaving an abusive parent, or removing a child from a place where that child's innocence is being destroyed. I am with you and give you every guidance in this very serious matter. I want your children protected, and I will help you to do this.

There are also cases, though, where a parent simply refuses his or her responsibility. These souls want to be children themselves and seek an extension to their childhood. Dear ones, your childhood is a time of formation. When it is over, you must understand that I expect you to put childish things behind you and spend your time doing My will. If I have gifted you with children, I expect you to parent them with all love, patience, and responsibility. This is your holy duty and your duty comes first. It is in this way, by the completion of your duty, that you obtain Heaven. I want the family supported. I want each one of My souls to focus on their family and always put family interests first. Be attentive to your earthly spouse. Consider your marriage as the primary consideration for every decision you make. I have given you your spouse so that you can lead each other to Heaven and help each other obtain a higher degree of holiness than you could have obtained without the participation in this sacramental union. So always view your marriage as a holy covenant, in which I participate. If you do this, My children, I will have no more concerns about families, because your children will be honored and loved, as I intended them to be.

August 29, 2003
Jesus

The love I feel bursts out from My Eucharistic heart. I cannot contain it. For such a time now, I have watched My children falter and err. I have seen them behave in such a way that they bring great pain and damage to their souls. Because they do not turn to Me, I cannot heal them and counsel them as I long to do. Thus they stumble on through their lives, repeating the same patterns and falling deeper into sin. Because of their pain, they inflict pain on others. Children, if I am describing you, I tell you now, it is time to stop. I am calling a halt to your destructive behavior, and I am giving you a unique opportunity. Come back to Me now, My little lost soul, and I will lift all punishment due you. Repent and throw yourself into My arms. I will forgive you immediately. I have already done so. But in order to heal and to be comfortable in Heaven, you must repent and seek My forgiveness. You must come to Me to seek My forgiveness. You must come and get it from Me. I am here, in the tabernacle. Come to Me here and I will forgive all sin. I will make you as pure as if you had never sinned. My children, all in Heaven are awed at the scope of this promise. I want you to consider that this is an opportunity you should take advantage of. You will not have forever to do this. You do not have eternity on this earth. You have made mistakes and left the path to Heaven. I implore you to return to Me now, before it is too late for you. You must understand that your soul can be lost. If you linger too long in mortal sin, My child, you will take to it as a child takes to a bad habit. The time to return is now. I come to you in these words because My love can no longer remain unrequited. It longs to comfort and console, and you, My child, are in need of comfort and consolation. If you let Me tell you of My love for you, you will begin to understand how irreplaceable you are to Me. Your gifts, strengths, and skills were given to you so that you could further My Kingdom on earth, as an obedient and loving child looks after the interests of his father. But, for some time now, you have not done that. You have looked after your own interests, either through the slavery of addiction or through the quest for worldly goods and sensual experiences. My child, I know you feel this is your business and perhaps you feel you hurt only yourself. I tell you now that you are My child, I love you, and I take it very personally when you hurt yourself. I am telling you now to stop. Stop any behavior that is separating you from Me. Are you unsure what those behaviors are? Come to Me, here in the tabernacle, and I will tell you exactly which behaviors I refer to. You know already, as you read these words. You must not trade these behaviors for your eternal life, My child. You must not. That is the second part of the reason why I compel you to return to Me. The third reason you must change your behavior is because I need you. I am your God, the God of All, and truly I say to you, I need you. There are souls in your world that only you can save. You must be working for Me to save them, because I have to tell you how and you have to be listening. So please, little souls of My heart, come to Me now, because the first part of the reason compelling your return is that I love you and separation from you is making My heart ache with loneliness.

August 29, 2003
Jesus

I wish to speak to My children about their speech. My children, does your speech accurately reflect who you wish to become? I want you to desire holiness. And I want your speech to be the conversation of a holy soul. My child, I know that you struggle and often do not feel holy. We allow this to protect your humility. But I want you to speak as though you have achieved the level of holiness I desire for you. "Jesus, what do You mean?" I hear you ask. I am with you, and you are with Me. Your speech must display or illustrate our unity. Do not think that you have gained this unity but must keep it hidden. My child, that would threaten part of our goal for you, which is that others look at you and see Me. Others must also listen to you and hear Me. As a holy exercise, and in that same spirit of practice we have adopted, I want you to listen to what you say. Listen to your voice. And understand that I am also listening with you. Pay attention to your words, of course, but also to your tone and the inflections you use. Are your words, tone, and inflections meant to convey love? Do they accurately represent God, whom you carry within yourself? You will find, I am certain, that at times you will see that your speech does not reflect Me. Do not be upset by this, little learning soul. That is why we are checking. We are leaving no stone unturned to secure your beautiful reward in Heaven. So when you identify something in your speech that you feel I would not approve of, ask Me how to say that thing differently. My child, you have been reading My words and hearing them in your heart. I wanted this for you because I wanted you to know Me. After all, I am your Savior. It is fitting that you be intimately acquainted with Me. So now that you have listened to Me, I want you to speak to others as I speak to you. Let us review. I speak the truth. Always. Children, do not tell lies. To lie is to sin and remember that sin requires repentance. I speak with great kindness. I am gentle, but I do not withhold the truth, My child, because I fear your anger. If you are called upon to correct someone, do so. Counsel a friend or loved one in moral matters if you feel they are mistaken. Ask Me if I want this from you and I will tell you. Often I prompt a soul to correct a loved one. I understand that this calls for courage but I will see that you do not lack courage if you are following My will. Speak with great love and gentleness and speak the truth. Often, hearing the truth will anger a soul. Remain calm and loving in the face of this anger and know that people were and are often angry with Me.

Children, do not spread unpleasantness about others, either factual or not. Say nothing unless you speak to protect another. Usually you should remain quiet about the sins of your sisters and brothers, as you have enough of your own to be busy about. Speak of kindnesses, sacrifices, and loving acts that brought you joy. Focus on the many, many good qualities of others. Remember that if a soul is not united to Me, that soul feels a gaping emptiness, a loneliness, and a sadness. Dearest children who are close to My heart, have compassion and mercy as I have had compassion and mercy for you.

I am your God. For every kindness you show to others, you will receive a personal kindness from Me. Guard your speech well, little one. Let your speech bring only Me to others. I will help you. Together we will be certain that your speech profits Heaven.

August 29, 2003
Jesus

My children, would you like to know how to please Me? Would you like to know what consoles Me and comforts Me in the face of widespread disobedience and hatred? Humility comforts Me. Humility consoles Me. Truly, the humility of My chosen souls softens My heart and deflects punishment from a cold world, undeserving of the mercy of its God. My children, the closer you come to Me, the more you recognize My goodness. Your intellect will automatically compare your holiness to My perfection and the result is humility. This is good. Do not fear the knowledge that you are imperfect and must improve. That is the journey, My child. When I walked your earth, people called Me "Teacher." I am still a Teacher and I am teaching you now. Like many teachers, I teach by showing you how to do a thing. My child, when you read Scripture you will become familiar with how I lived. You must do this daily and through Scripture you will learn about Me. Days will pass and your life will unfold before you and you will find yourself becoming Me. You will watch your heart be moved with pity for humanity, as Mine was moved. You will accept hurts with dignity and understanding, seeking no revenge. Yes, you will change. And change is what we seek together. You cannot stay the same and become holy. That would be impossible. The very call to holiness, and I know that you, My little soul, understand that it is to you I speak, demands change. You are in the process of becoming a saint and that is what I have predestined for you.

My child, you must not be jealous of the holiness of another. I have given each of My children different gifts, suited to the tasks I require from them. It would hardly do for Me to give you the spiritual gifts of your neighbor, and then expect you to complete tasks that require different gifts. My way is perfect. My plan is perfect. I am perfect. You want to be My friend, My little soul. I am the only way for you. Soon you will realize this but I want you to realize and accept this right now. Heed My words and take My hand and I will put you on the path I have laid out for you. It will feel right to you as it has been designed only for you by your God, who knows you with a perfect and complete knowledge. My will for you includes peace, and peace will settle upon you as you begin to follow Me. My child, I have many enemies and few friends. May I call you My friend? Will you stand by Me during these days of disobedience? Please, join your heart to My heart and join your will to My will. Together we can save souls. My gratitude flows out to you and you will never understand the power of a grateful God. Truly, I am a slave to My children who serve Me, despite difficulty and ridicule. If I were dragging My cross through your town, surrounded by angry mobs, would you watch from a safe distance? Or would you stand with Me, taking a share of the weight of that cross? My child, do not fear if you answered from weakness. If you come to Me and let Me change you, I can make of you the most loyal and courageous servant. I am with you as you struggle to detach from the world and join My loyal followers. I am putting you together so that you may draw strength from each other. Be at peace. I am God and I call My world back to Me.

September 1, 2003
Jesus

I am with My children. My presence is silent but constant. I am directing many of the seemingly unimportant events in your lives, so that My will can be accomplished. My children are practicing faith, and that pleases Me. But My protection is so great that My children could have an infinite amount of faith in Me and still more would be justified. My faithful ones, who are struggling to serve Me and be holy, please trust Me for I am with you. I have pledged My protection to you and I will not leave you vulnerable. Offer Me small little prayers when you are frightened or unsure and I will place My calming hands upon you, steadying and reassuring you. You will look back at this time of service to Me and you will be so grateful that you said "yes" to your God. My children, you will look upon so many souls sharing eternity with you who would be absent if not for your service. Can you imagine the joy you will share with these souls? So be brave and continue in My service, walking the path I have illuminated before you. It is there you will find your peace and your key to eternity.

For today, I want to warn you about a snare or a trap. My children often want to do big things for Me, and truly, big things are necessary and big things will be asked of you. But your holiness lies in the small, dear soul. It is in the small unseen tasks and duties that I whisper to your soul, that I mold a bit here, reform a bit there. You do not feel these changes because they are so subtle, but changes occur, My child, in the small things. So do not begrudge Me the mundane. Complete small, humble acts with love and patience so that I may do My work in your soul as quickly as possible. Yes, we are going to save many souls, and bring the world back to the light, but we are going to do that one soul at a time. Right now, I am starting with you. So give yourself to Me that I may change the world. Together, you and I must perfect your beautiful soul, insuring that it reaches its fullest potential, both here and in Heaven. Do you trust Me, My child? Trust can be difficult, but this is one time when you can step out in complete trust and confidence because I will not let you fall. I am here, ready to save you. I have waited for this day, My child, for so long. My heart aches with love for you and watching you read these words creates an even stronger love in My heart. I will take care of you and you can close your eyes and rest in My heart. You have suffered because of the distance between us. Often you did not know where the pain originated, but I assure you, the pain began when you turned away from Me. Our standards must be high now, as I desire your happiness. I want you to remain in My heart, where I place you today. I will help, My dear child. You are infinitely precious to Me and if you show Me the smallest desire, I can keep you firmly joined to Me, despite the winds that try to tear you away. Have every confidence that the smallest bit of faith will be rewarded in these days of difficulty. Heaven is united with earth in this mission of salvation for souls. All assistance is available to each soul who seeks to be saved. Be at peace, now, My little soul. I am holding you tightly.

September 1, 2003
Jesus

I want My children to be calm. Even in My service, My children tend to rush to and fro, as though this life were a race. My children, when you are hurrying, I cannot help you to listen. I may want to whisper something to your soul, an instruction, a bit of encouragement, or a word of love if you are being maligned. Often, though, you are moving so quickly that your heart and mind are already on the next task, leaving the current task incomplete or improperly executed. So, slow down, dear ones, that your Jesus might be truly united in your work and in your recreation. I do not like to hurry, and you carry Me with you. There are times, My child, when I wish to work through you to guide or console a soul in distress. If you are hurried, you will miss My cue and the soul will remain without necessary consolation and guidance. Children, this is the state of affairs all over your world at this time. Do you notice that loneliness and despair are everywhere? Children, you will not find loneliness and despair where I am. Indeed, even in the most wretched of circumstances, if I am present, you will see eyes that smile and offer kindness, and you will see great hope, even in the face of suffering and death. So what is missing in your world? I am missing. Few souls allow Me to work through them. When I am allowed, you will see hope begin to flourish again. Faces will be more at peace and joy will flow naturally from one soul to another. I will put such joy in your faces that you will be unable to conceal your unity with Me. Crosses will feel lighter and hold great meaning. Children, I have so much to offer you, both in these words and in My constant presence in your lives. So do not turn away, even for a day. Draw closer to Me, that we may proceed. What feels difficult to you, anticipating changes in your life, will come easily. That is another promise I make to you. Such will be our union that you will consult Me on everything. Your life will reflect Heaven. Souls will be drawn to you because of this and you will be equal to the represent-ation of your God. Be joyful now because My plan has been set in motion and all creation awaits My coming. You will see changes in your world and you will understand and welcome these changes as a sign that your Jesus has heard the prayers of His children and is responding in love. Be calm, My child, in the face of all difficulties because I am steering the direction of the world now. I want My children practicing a quiet and thoughtful approach to every single day, and every hour in that day. Your thoughts, of course, should be turned to Me whenever possible. A small prayer, a sentence in your heart, is enough to ignite the faith and trust in your soul, which returns calmness to you. In this way, when upsetting events occur in your life, you will be comfortable confronting troubles in unity with Me, your Jesus. How different you will find life. How peaceful and joyful. I want the times when you are hurried to be rare. So much so, that you will note the rushed feeling and immediately seek to alert Me that you are not recollected. I will then restore your quietness so that you serve Me thoroughly.

September 1, 2003
Jesus

My child, with such gratitude I view your efforts. I am here, waiting in the tabernacle to thank you and encourage you. You are trying to serve Me in your life and it is not always easy to do this. Until a complete union or surrender occurs, you continue to wrestle with the pull of the world and worldly attractions and distractions. This creates conflict in you because I am calling you in another direction. This conflict makes you feel discouraged, dear one, but you should not allow this feeling. There is not growth without some bit of discomfort. So, when you feel unsettled and you long for old habits, remember that you used those habits to console yourself in emptiness. I am now filling that emptiness for you so you do not need to rely on these things anymore. Worldly habits or addictions did not make you happy, My little soul. You felt unrest and bitterness without Me. Now, with Me, you are beginning to experience true peace, the peace which comes from Heaven. This is a sign that your soul is directing the movement and action of your body, which is how man is intended to live. The body is under your dominion, or the dominion of your soul, and the soul, your precious and irreplaceable soul, is under My dominion. In this way, in this small corner, the world is as it should be. You belong to Me, My child, and I have defended you fiercely, despite your temporary indifference to Me. We will keep moving forward now with our movement toward unity. You may feel as though you are moving quite swiftly in these spiritual matters. Do not fear this haste as I am personally determining the speed at which I need you to ascend. In days past, perhaps your conversion would be more gentle and leisurely. I do not will that now and it is not what I require. I need My soldiers prepared quickly. Because I am God, and all created things bow to Me, I can do this with a soul like yours who seeks to assist Me and please Me.

My child, never be afraid of holiness. When you doubt, look to your duty and remain calm until I desire to erase your doubts. You will carry small crosses of fear and doubt at times, but that is, again, more practice, and these little exercises are good for your soul. Make small acts of faith to Me and the doubts will lose their power to distract you from My service during your days.

I am with you, My little souls, and we have

discussed exactly what I mean when I say that. You are with Me and we move purposefully through your life together. Look for opportunities to serve Me in the people I place in your path. If you sense that I need you to assist a soul, let your spirit go quiet while I place the proper inspirations in your heart and mind. Then you may respond to the need in this soul for Me, and My word, My presence, will have been achieved. Dear little soul, so willing to serve Me, can you imagine your world if even a small number begin to live this way? Your world would change and that is what I am seeking to accomplish. Be at peace. Your God is pleased.

September 2, 2003
Jesus

I want My children to be at peace. You know this, children, as I often say this to you. Today, I am going to teach you how to keep peace in your hearts at all times. My children, when a parent rocks a child and sings a soft lullaby, the child knows peace, so much so, that the child often closes his little eyes and falls effortlessly into a peaceful sleep. My children, I am holding you in My arms. I am rocking you gently. Many times throughout your day, I want you to stop what you are doing for a brief moment and close your eyes. I will momentarily soothe your soul with that very same gentleness and, if only for a moment, you will know the sleep of peace. You will be fully aware in your senses, of course, but your soul will rest in complete union with Me and your entire being will be restored and balanced. My children, this is how I intend to keep you at peace. You must fear nothing, not even death. Why would death frighten a soul who is destined for eternity with Me? You are merely coming home, My child, and the brief moments of death are an almost instantaneous transit time. No, do not fear death. That will distract you from life and we want no distractions from the completion of your earthly duties.

My children, are you attempting to remain with Me throughout your day? Remember that you are practicing and trying to consider My presence and how I would speak. You are asking Me often what I would like you to do. This is the way, children. Do you see the changes I am making in your soul? Do you see the difference in how you view your brothers and sisters? You understand now that I am making these changes and that you can trust Me to keep My word. We are making progress, My child, and that pleases Me. This world will shift the smallest bit each time a soul moves closer to Me in trust. I want you to feel joy, My child. Your world is not at peace, but you must be. I am placing peace in your souls and the world is going to draw it from you, much the way an infant draws nourishment from her mother. That is why I am asking you to come to Me often in your day. As the world draws peace from you to quiet the terrible unrest, I will replace it in you. So do not worry or fret because the world takes your peace. It is for the world I give it, and I have an endless store with which to replenish you. Do you begin to see the depth of My plan? I need many souls to help Me and right now I do not have enough. So we must take My plea to the world so that all souls of good will may answer and assist Me. It is fair and just, My child, that each be given the opportunity to answer for themselves. I am asking and each soul must answer. In their soul, they know they are being asked to choose and they make the choice. I am God. I know all. I need souls. There is no hiding from Me. If a soul rejects Me now, it is finished. You cannot reject your God and claim Heaven as your inheritance. Be at peace, My little one. Your God moves to right all wrongs.

September 2, 2003
Jesus

My children, these words are lessons in love. I seek to teach you that love is sacrifice. The two words, love and sacrifice, are nearly interchangeable from the heavenly perspective. If you love someone, you are willing to sacrifice for their well-being. In earthly terms, if you value or love a thing, you are willing to work, save, and plan to acquire that thing. If you place that same concept into heavenly terms, you can take a virtue, such as the virtue of obedience. If obedience is a valuable thing to you, a desired thing, you will work, sacrifice, and be patient until you can acquire this virtue. It is the very same with all of the heavenly virtues. I want you to value and put great emphasis on these heavenly virtues. I, your Jesus, am saying to you, truly, you will need to have these things to acquire Heaven. You believe Me, and know that I speak only the truth. So you must begin to concentrate on the acquisition of these virtues. You must sacrifice to achieve these virtues. You are practicing and these virtues are becoming more second nature. You see them in your daily lives and your behaviors are changing. We are working on patience. We are working on trust. We work on fortitude. You are becoming kinder and more compassionate. My children, all is going as it should be. I tell you that you are destined for great holiness and you will achieve this holiness if you remain united to Me. And you will do so because I will protect you.

Children, do not seek to further or advance the opinion others have of you. It is irrelevant. Please spend no time at all wondering or worrying about this. Worldly opinions change with the wind and a person could think well of you one day and slander you the next. You must not rely on these opinions for your peace because, as you have learned, you will be disappointed. Instead, rely on Me, who does not change. My opinion of you remains steady. I will always love you. I will always seek your betterment and well-being. I will always help you and consider your interests My own. So spend no time entertaining grief that the world does not appreciate you. You will be appreciated in Heaven, and indeed this is already the case. Heaven is pleased with holy souls and seeks to assist them. Your heavenly friends will do more good for you than worldly friends who are not rooted in God. Be at peace, dear ones, as I will warn you when another seeks to harm you. I will protect you. Be assured that if you follow Me, all that occurs in your life will be for the advancement of your soul and the virtues I wish your soul to house. If you are ill, particularly, spend your days with Me and I can show you heights of holiness that will leave you breathless. I work with great energy in the soul of someone who suffers physically. Trust Me, please, with everything, for I am caring for you lovingly.

September 2, 2003
Jesus

Today we must talk about purity. My children, lack of purity is a very significant problem in your world. I search for purity and only find it in rare pockets. Because the tolerance for impurity is so profound, we are going to have to work very hard on this problem. Purity must be restored to every aspect of existence on earth. First, I speak of purity of dress. Do not dress in such a way as to indicate that you will behave sinfully. Dress as though you are a servant of Mine and seek My will. It is never My will to dress in clothes that lead others astray. Children, you know what I am referring to and I want this to stop. Modesty must be restored. Use these words often in your speech to remind people that purity and modesty are to be valued and applauded.

Next I speak of purity of speech. You must speak like a Christian, keeping your language worthy of your soul and the work I am doing in your soul. Language is often the method used by the enemy to spread the contagion of impurity. Use words that glorify Me. If you use My name to curse, My child, I will be personally offended and you will have to make amends to Me.

My children, I ask that you take offense to impurity in every form of entertainment. No longer should you sit idly while those who claim to be artists desecrate Me. Defend Me. I am your God. I want to hear your cry of outrage if I am maligned. If you, who know Me so well, do not defend Me, who will? Speak with immediacy when you are offended by forms of entertainment such as music, television, writings, or art. Do not let the enemy think he has overcome all Christian thought. I will reward you beyond your understanding for efforts against the scourge of impurity. Your youth are being poisoned this way and we must change this with decision now.

Impure thoughts can be more difficult because often you do not will these and they are a cross for you. If we change this type of dress, speech, and entertainment, though, you will see the volume of impure thoughts diminishing quickly. It is the constant reference to the impure that sparks these thoughts. Nevertheless, My little ones, push the impure thoughts from your head calmly. Distract yourself by looking away from objects of impurity. Ask for My help and I will assist you. Prayer and a consistent participation in the sacraments will arm you against these attacks on your purity.

I want you to understand that living in the world as it is will not be considered a valid excuse for either behaving impurely or leading others to impurity. I hold each soul accountable for actions committed knowingly. Parents, guide your children in these matters and set positive examples. Children, obey your parents in these matters and know that I am with you always. We will work on this together and together we will overcome impurity with a dedicated and purposeful outcry. I am with you and will show you exactly what I am asking for in this regard. My children, I want to thank you, now and always, for your obedience and service to Me. Your every effort will be preserved and rewarded. When your sins are presented to Me, I will turn My head away. That is what comes from your effort to serve Me. Be at peace now and do not let past sins of impurity disturb you. All is forgiven and My memory is short when it comes to My servants.

September 3, 2003
Jesus

I want to talk to souls about love of neighbor. My children, people are precious. Each and every person on this earth is of infinite value to Me and to My heavenly plan. But often the value is overlooked because of a worldly view of life. If I have placed a person on your earth, I intend that the person be adequately fed. You must proceed from that assumption. Dear little soul, so earnestly trying to serve Me, if you know of a soul who is not fed, perhaps I intended that you feed that person, and that is why I reveal that person's plight to you. Be thoughtfully considerate when you hear of a person or a group of people who are hungry. Then, ask Me what it is I am asking that you do in the matter. Perhaps I am merely looking for prayers. Perhaps I am making you aware of the great blessings that have been bestowed upon you. Or perhaps I am asking that you share in your wealth and support My workers who are attempting to feed these souls. Again, perhaps I am asking you to be one of those souls who ministers directly to unfortunates, who lack the barest necessities for human existence. You have a role. You must ask Me to reveal it to you so that souls on earth are not housed in bodies that cannot develop because they lack food. I see every need of every soul on earth. It is My intention that My children serve each other and in this way achieve holiness. Many are starving today in your world. My children, this is yet another symptom of the Age of Disobedience, a time in which more souls defy Me than serve me. I do not want people starving. Ask Me what you can do.

Children, I want you to think of the person you like least in this world. You have many reasons for disliking this person. You have been hurt, possibly, and it is difficult to forget that pain. Perhaps you fear that person would hurt you again if you were to attempt reconciliation. I am asking you, though, to love your neighbor. "Jesus," you ask, "what do You want from me?" I tell you, My child, that I fear for your spiritual development if you are harboring bitterness, whatever its source. Because bitterness often originates from another soul, I want you to examine any bitterness in your heart closely. If indeed you do, and you can identify this person who has caused you harm, I want you to spend this day praying for that individual. My child, ask Me to have mercy on this person. My just wrath is a terrible thing to behold and you would not like it to be directed at you. Therefore, you must also seek to spare others this destiny. Love of neighbor delights Me. Mercy and compassion given freely to others delights Me. Forgiveness? I need not even tell you about the happiness that comes to Me when I see souls offering forgiveness to each other. Understand, little souls, that I place people in your path with an intention and with a hope, a heavenly hope. Do not be quick to run from a soul, simply because he does not please you. Consider My will and be certain to ask Me if I have a heavenly task for you with regard to each person. It is in this way I will bring love to each soul, through love of neighbor.

September 3, 2003
Jesus

My children, often examine your intentions, seeking purity of your actions. I want you to act from your heart and when results are not what you hoped for, come back to Me and I will console you. Often in your life you will obey Me with a predetermined notion of what the outcome will be. My goal or desired outcome may be different than what you expect. Do not allow yourself to be disappointed when events in your life turn out differently than you thought they would. My will is being served if you are doing your best to obey Me. Concern yourself only with what I am asking of you. In this way you can walk in gladness, with a light and happy spirit, because you are serving your God and doing your part to bring about My Kingdom. My child, how grateful I am to you. And what kinship is sent your way from your heavenly comrades. Be joyful.

Look to Me when you are faced with decisions. At times you will need to look closely at why you are choosing a course of action. I am warning you about this because I want you to begin to discern your own motives. In this way you can avoid acting from human weakness and seek only the divine or holy in your life. The enemy seeks to interfere with your decision to serve Me but we will not allow any more diversions from your heavenly path. We will together seek only heavenly motivations and your every task and project will further both My will and your soul. My yoke is easy and My burden is light. I allow crosses for your humility and improvement. If you feel a cross is too heavy, you may ask Me for relief. I will not be offended by this, My child. And unless it is necessary for you to retain that cross, I will remove either the cross itself, or the weight from it. We are united and we can discuss everything. Often you rail against your circumstances but do not come to Me to object. Of what use is complaining to others? They cannot lift your cross or even ease your burdens. Talk to Me and listen to others. In that way you will not fall into sins of the tongue, which do great damage in this world. I am here, waiting to listen to your every complaint. Every sorrow you suffer finds a warm, comfortable place in My heart and, truly, when you share sorrow with Me it is diminished. I want to give you eyes of Heaven. I want you to see your life, this world, and its people, with these heavenly eyes so that you will begin to respond like Me, your Jesus, who loves you so dearly. My child, I am offering this new vision to you. Will you accept this wonderful gift from Me? Truly, you will be astonished at how this viewpoint will change your life. Most of what disturbed you in the past will simply fade away, out of your line of vision, because it will hold such little importance for you. Do you want this? I am so hopeful that you will say "yes." I want so badly to show you the world from My eyes. I can teach you such great things, My dear one. And if you share My vision, we can talk as freely as one soul. Be this for Me, please. Allow Me to dictate your perspective.

September 3, 2003
Jesus

I wish to tell My souls about the joys of Heaven. My children, there is no bitterness in Heaven. Bitterness and distress are not intended for you, even on earth. These are experienced by every soul at some time during their earthly time, but souls should not see bitterness and distress as the defining characteristics of their life. My child, if you feel you struggle often with these destructive patterns, you must spend time with Me. I am the Divine Healer. I can remove all hardness from your hearts so that you are liberated to love with no barrier. In that way, you become a more effective servant because you are open to receiving love, as well as giving love. My child, I do not wish to add to your grief. You will not pursue a relationship with Me and be disappointed. Run joyfully into this relationship with Me because you are guaranteed to succeed. I, the God of All, am making this guarantee to you. You fear failure, perhaps because in the past you have failed. Consider, My dearest, that you may be attributing failure to yourself where none exists. Put another way, once you begin to walk in unity with Me, your God who loves you, you will see success and failure more clearly. What may have

*appeared to be failure to you in your past,
may look like success to you when viewed
from My eyes. I am looking at effort, not
result. The result of an effort is My affair
and you must leave that to Me. So, in the
name of reflection, look back now on your
life. Think of these things that haunt you
as failures. Did you try in these endeavors?
Did you often do your best? When you saw
a thing falling apart did you attempt to
change your approach? Perhaps your
failures were not failures at all. Perhaps
you were seeking and not finding. Be at
peace. You have found Me now and I will
bring you every success, regardless of how
the world views your endeavors. You are
succeeding now, My beloved child, because
you are sitting quietly while I minister to
your soul and heal your wounds. Yes, we
are a success. Together, we do not fail.
Today is your beginning. Start freshly with
Me right now and all possibilities open
before you. Your heart begins to ache and
this feels almost like pain, but a pain you
would not run away from. This is divine
love, little soul. This is how it feels when
you allow your God to love you. You feel a
longing. Your heart looks around initially,
because your heart cannot determine the
object of its longing. This is the beginning
of becoming a saint, My child. These first
stirrings are a desire for unity with your*

God. This desire grows stronger and stronger and you can measure your holiness, if such a thing were necessary, by this aching. I tell you solemnly, with all of My Godly majesty, you will achieve fulfillment of this longing in Heaven.

September 4, 2003
Jesus

I have come to cleanse souls. Much as a mother cleans her house, My child, I am cleaning and organizing your soul. If you have been away from Me, we must be busy. Events in your life, from your past, must be looked at now in a different way. This is an important task, and that is why I am spending time on it with you. Events can leave marks on your heart when you are not praying. Hence, My goal. To clean these marks and leave a heart that gives and receives love freely. When you pray, My child, I help you to sift through the experiences occurring in your life. Perhaps you have a disappointment today. Taken alone, without My assistance, you might feel down, sad and discouraged. If pride is a problem for you, and many suffer from pride, you might not share your sadness and disappointment with even another soul. It remains on your poor heart and, after a time, this turns to bitterness. Now, earthly life being what it is, and human beings being flawed, as they are in their search for perfection, you encounter yet another disappointment or betrayal. Pride asserts itself and again you do not adequately share your grief. Another patch of disappointment turns to bitterness and covers another area of your poor little heart. My child, when this process continues, you have a heart enclosed in bitterness. A heart needs love, in the same way your lungs need oxygen. Your heart was designed this way, dearest, and if your heart is enclosed, the love is blocked off. How handicapped you are in the spiritual sense. How it grieves Me to see you so disturbed and unhappy. My little one, I am coming to clean every mark from your heart so that you will love freely, as I love. Do not think this is an impossible task. I am Jesus. I am God. I can cleanse your heart in no time at all if you are willing to let Me. I will restore order to your soul, I will adjust your thinking, and I will place the kind of love in your heart that is so genuine and abundant that this love reaches your eyes. All who see you will experience this love and know it is from Me. My child, My child, how grieved I am that those who should have loved you did not. I am sorry that anything hurtful has ever happened to you. But you must see that we benefit from suffering. Let Me show you how to make everything bad that has hurt you work to your benefit. Talk to Me. Pour it out to Me and I will grant you a peace, a forgiveness, and an order to all that has occurred in your life. I must tell you that when you have a disappointment in your life and you bring it to Me, I immediately help you to understand and recover. It could be that your recovery time is going to be a period of growth, during which you and I will grow closer and more dependent on each other. Would you begrudge Me that time, My child, if I needed it to make you into the kind of saint I need for certain work destined for you? Of course you would not because you are searching for My will. If you pray, I will not let you suffer unnecessarily. That is a pledge I make to you today. Please take that sentence to heart and hold it closely. If you pray to Me, I will not let you suffer unnecessarily. Ask Me for relief of your suffering, and if it is not benefitting you, I will remove it. Be at peace now and tell Me of everything that occurs in your life. Together we will ensure that no further blocks fall upon your tender heart.

September 4, 2003
Jesus

My children, I would like you to become dependable friends to Me. I want to rely on you. You are wondering what that means so I will tell you. It is true, I am walking with you. I am sharing your life and worries. Your business is My business and I help you with everything. No detail is too small for you to share with Me and seek assistance. You find Me there, always. You know I never leave you. You are only being wise to have this confidence in Me, My child, because it is a confidence that rests on the rock of truth. I am that rock and I am that truth. In the same way, with every allowance made for both your frail humanity and your earthly duties, I want you to walk with Me. I would like to know that you will come to Me every day in prayer. We begin a journey together and then you disappear from Me. I remain with you, of course. I am your God and will not leave you. But we must finish the work we begin. Do not be haphazard about your time with Me. You are busy and I understand because it is often I who have given you your duties. But if you do not have time to pray to Me, there is something amiss in your life and I want it sorted out immediately. I need you. You are My friend and I need My friends to be faithful right now. So do not come and go anymore. Please, stay united to Me so that we can work together on the tasks left undone by others. My child, you must understand that when you come to Me in prayer, if only for a moment, I am consoled. My heart is comforted, which allows Me to give you untold graces, of course, but also, your prayer allows Me to soften My justice toward others who never seek Me. When you meet Me face to face, you will see clearly every happiness you have caused Me. I need you and so appreciate any fidelity offered to Me. If only for the sake of repayment you should come to Me often, as I reward each prayer, each glance, each petition even, beyond anything you might imagine. Please do not worry if you do not feel like you think you should feel. My child, how does a saint feel when that saint is laboring on earth? Very often, My saintly souls feel tired. They feel tired because they are laboring. But they also feel determined and these saintly souls come back to Me in prayer, even though they do not feel holy every moment. Do not let your feelings dictate your prayer time. Imagine a marriage where the two people only served each other in times of romantic love. I need not tell you that the marriage would be doomed. It is the very same with your relationship to Me. Serve Me always, regardless of how you feel. Do you imagine, My child, that you will come to Me in prayer and I will turn away? Will I say, "Go away, you do not feel holy enough to talk to Me"? Does a husband say, "Go away, my wife, you do not feel enough love for me"? How ridiculous. It is particularly in those times when you do not feel holy that I must listen to you and soothe and love you. We are to be close friends, which means we will be friends in times of spiritual joy. But, as close friends, our friendship will become even more precious, more valuable, and more indispensable during times when you feel a spiritual dryness. Be at peace. I seek to explain everything to you now, leaving no questions and no hurtful marks on your heart.

September 4, 2003
Jesus

My children, I am not aggressive, unless one of My own is under attack and needs My protection. Normally, I am gentle and slow to anger. You will find Me a calm companion to your days. I see events clearly. I am able to read the intentions in the souls of others so I am the one to consult when you have difficulty. If you are needlessly upsetting yourself with a person, I will tell you. I am very patient with My children, particularly when they have turned away from Me. I will send many chosen souls to them in an attempt to get their attention. But I cannot will their response because they own their will. I would not give a gift to you and then take it away. If a soul rejects you, you must be at peace. Consult Me often when you are working with a soul. Pray for him. Love him. Show him by your example what it is to live the life of a follower. Are you calm? Are you peaceful? Those qualities are very attractive to a soul who is experiencing distress. You must convey to a struggling soul that the answer for everything is with Me. He may say that you don't understand that his problems are grave, complex, and unsolvable. He may cite reasons why he does not follow Me, always blaming others.

The answers are all with Me. There is no reason to reject God. No excuse will gain pardon on judgment day. I have never shown a soul unkindness or cruelty. I deserve love, loyalty and respect. Understand My power and you will begin to understand My gentleness. Foolish souls equate gentleness with weakness. It is the truly strong who are wise enough to be gentle. So treat your brothers and sisters gently, particularly those who are not united to Me. They wound so easily. They do not have Me to console them when they are hurt. Can you imagine such loneliness? Would you like to return to a world that did not include Me in any way? Do not even imagine such a thing because I have promised not to let you go. Truly, I will not. But be compassionate.

My child, have no fear about your future. Do not spend time imagining what will happen to you and what I will ask of you. This type of dreaming is not productive. Rather spend this time meditating on My Passion. That type of exercise is productive and will allow Me to reveal Myself further to you. Our union will be deepened and you will gain much. You will have the joy of knowing that when others ran, you remained. I cannot convey to you the joy this will bring to you. Let Me say that throughout all eternity such knowledge will delight you. It is difficult for you to imagine eternity, but the closer you come to Me, the more real it becomes. Your exile from us on earth is a testing time. Do not fail the test by wasting opportunities. Do not fail the test by spending your today feeling badly about yesterday. Did I not assure you that My memory is short? Your failings will be forgotten, child. Only do not turn away from Me now. I place great trust in you because I, your God and Savior, know you. I see straight into your humanity and know each capability. You are able to do great things, My little servant, but not without Me. You were formed and designed to work with Me. Without Me your work will remain undone because you will not be able to identify it, much less accomplish it. When this occurs, and I tell you I do not expect this from you, others must carry heavier loads and do your work as well as their own. It is for this reason that My true servants carry heavy burdens. But, My will is being accomplished and My time of renewal draws near. Have no fear. I am reclaiming My world.

September 5, 2003
Jesus

I want My children prepared. Today it is My wish to help My children understand the times in which they live. Children, you are close to My heart. You were put on earth for this time so that you could serve Me and assist Me in ushering in My Kingdom. The time of darkness takes its final souls as I prepare to return. The result is assured, as I often remind you. What is not assured is how many souls will choose light and how many souls will choose darkness. Be influential, My children. In your quiet, calm holiness, with eyes that reflect all of My kindness, be influential. Others must see more and more of My peaceful children, standing firmly in My presence. In this way, they will be attracted to Me. That is our mission. My words here in these pages are intended to assist you in this process, the process of holiness. And holiness is a process of becoming, My dear ones. Will you ever say you are holy enough? Of course not. While you remain on earth, I will have divine work for you, both in your soul and in your world. Never content yourself that you have done a good job yesterday. To content yourself in spiritu-

ality is to begin the slide back into the world. Our standards are high but you are able and again, together, we succeed. I am with you daily, hourly, and through everything you experience. Please give glory to our Father in Heaven for His countless mercies during this time. He has been disobeyed in every area of humanity, and even now His concern is for His children. Dear ones, I have prepared you well. You are responding to My grace and becoming saints. How pleased I am with your progress, and also with the zeal with which you seek to share My words. I am calling and you are answering. I give you tasks and you complete these tasks. When this happens, all is at peace in your soul. Do not be afraid. Fear nothing. Did I not assure you of My power? Come to Me often and discuss every concern, every joy and every decision with Me. In this way you will be certain you serve Me and not the world. I wait for you often during the day to glance My way, and the moment you do, graces are sent down upon you. I will preserve you in My grace. I will open the path before you. I will count your enemies as My own and your interests will be Mine. We are united. Always proceed from that fact. You and I are one. Truly, you carry Me, your Jesus, your Savior, with you, My child. I leave you with that statement for now because you must live your whole life by that one fact. Be at peace, to serve My Kingdom.

September 5, 2003
Blessed Mother

Dearest children, nestled in my Immaculate Heart, you must live your lives joyfully. Jesus, my beloved Son, has given you everything you need to become true servants. In order to have peace on this earth, you must serve Him, who is all light, all goodness. I am His Mother. I am also your Mother. Call on me often, little children of this world. I have helped many souls reach Heaven and I will help you. Confide your fears to me and I will console you. A motherly heart understands each weakness in her children and can help her children overcome habits that distract them from their union with God. Children, let me help you. Run to me when you fear you are not serving Jesus and I will lead you straight back to His holy path, the path He has marked especially for you. We are near you always, in everything. Truly, Heaven and earth are joined as never before. Take full advantage of this. Heaven is happy, dearest children, because God is there. But you can be happy on earth, also, because God is with you now. The more you seek Him, the more He will reveal Himself to you personally. All is well. We guard you and your loved ones without tiring, and you will see that your service to Heaven brings you joy and more joy. Be with Jesus, children.

September 5, 2003
Blessed Mother

My children, I am anxious that you persevere in your conversions. There are many graces available to you so that you stay this course to holiness. Because I am a Mother, your Mother, I anticipate dangers that threaten my little ones. Beware of spiritual pride. Jesus intends to bring each of you to a high level of holiness in a relatively short time. At no time should you think this holiness comes from you. Your faith, your love of God, is God's gift to you so do not hold yourself above your brothers and sisters who are not responding as fully and hence not receiving the same level of grace. My little one, you might wonder what it is you are contributing if everything is coming from Jesus. You are contributing your free will. You are contributing your time on earth. You are giving Jesus your heart and saying, "Yes, Jesus, I want to be a saint." Truly, little child of my heart, Jesus can do anything with a soul such as yours who has made a decision for Heaven. Consider yourself now a soldier in the army of light. I anoint you as such and you work only for goodness. Prayer is your weapon and you are armed with the holiness acquired through your obedience. No evil can prevail against you. Such is the power you wield with Jesus as your leader. Fear nothing. We are with you. Be available to accept your direction through prayer so that as times change we can instruct you in everything. We are always available to you. I bless you now and entrust you to my Son, Jesus Christ. Serve Him faithfully and you will know Heaven. How your loyalty will be rewarded. Truly, children, you will be overwhelmed with happiness. We have every answer, so bring every trouble to us. I am with you and seek to help you as a mother helps her children through difficult times. When you need me, dear ones, I will be there, with additional guidance for your time.

Prayer to the Heart of Jesus in the Most Blessed Sacrament

May the Heart of Jesus, in the Most Blessed Sacrament, be praised, adored, and loved with grateful affection, at every moment, in all the tabernacles of the world, even to the end of time. Amen.

Indulgence granted for this prayer in 1868 by Venerable Pope Pius IX.

Appendix

The Lay Apostolate of Jesus Christ the Returning King

We seek to be united to Jesus in our daily work, and through our vocations, in order to obtain graces for the conversion of sinners. Through our cooperation with the Holy Spirit, we will allow Jesus to flow through us to the world, bringing His light. We do this in union with Mary, our Blessed Mother, with the Communion of Saints, with all of God's holy angels and with our fellow lay apostles in the world.

Guidelines for Lay Apostles

As lay apostles of Jesus Christ the Returning King, we agree to perform our basic obligations as practicing Catholics. Additionally, we will adopt the following spiritual practices, as best we can:

1. **Allegiance Prayer** and **Morning Offering**, plus a brief prayer for the Holy Father
2. **Eucharistic Adoration**, one hour per week
3. **Prayer Group Participation**, monthly, at which we pray the Luminous Mysteries of the Holy Rosary and read the Monthly Message
4. **Monthly Confession**
5. Further, we will follow the example of Jesus Christ as set out in the Holy Scripture, treating all others with His patience and kindness.

Allegiance Prayer

Dear God in Heaven, I pledge my allegiance to You. I give You my life, my work and my heart. In turn, give me the grace of obeying Your every direction to the fullest possible extent. Amen.

Morning Offering

O Jesus, through the Immaculate Heart of Mary, I offer You the prayers, works, joys and sufferings of this day, for all the intentions of Your Sacred Heart, in union with the Holy Sacrifice of the Mass throughout the world, in reparation for my sins, and for the intentions of the Holy Father. Amen.

Prayer for the Holy Father

Blessed Mary, Mother of Jesus, protect our Holy Father, Francis, and bless his intentions.

Promise from Jesus to His Lay Apostles

May 12, 2005

Your message to souls remains constant. Welcome each soul to the rescue mission. You may assure each lay apostle that just as they concern themselves with My interests, I will concern Myself with theirs. They will be placed in My Sacred Heart and I will defend and protect them. I will also pursue complete conversion of each of their loved ones. So you see, the souls who serve in this rescue mission as My beloved lay apostles will know peace. The world cannot make this promise as only Heaven can bestow peace on a soul. This is truly Heaven's mission and I call every one of Heaven's children to assist Me. You will be well rewarded, My dear ones.

What about the Monthly Prayer Group?

Jesus asks us to form lay apostle prayer groups. He asks us to meet once each month to pray the Luminous Mysteries of the Holy Rosary and read the Monthly Message. A prayer group can be as small as two people within a family or as large as hundreds in a church.

Five Luminous Mysteries:

1. The Baptism of Jesus
2. The Wedding at Cana
3. The Proclamation of the Kingdom of God
4. The Transfiguration
5. The Institution of the Eucharist

Monthly Messages

For seven years Jesus gave Anne a message for the world on the first day of every month. Each month the apostolate reads and contemplates one of these monthly messages.

To receive the monthly messages you may access our website at **www.directionforourtimes.org** or call us at one of our offices to be placed on our mailing list.

We have also printed a book which contains all of the monthly messages. It can be purchased through our website as well.

Prayers taken from The Volumes

Prayers to God the Father

"What can I do for my Father in Heaven?"

"I trust You, God. I offer You my pain in the spirit of acceptance and I will serve You in every circumstance."

"God my Father in Heaven, You are all mercy. You love me and see my every sin. God, I call on You now as the Merciful Father. Forgive my every sin. Wash away the stains on my soul so that I may once again rest in complete innocence. I trust You, Father in Heaven. I rely on You. I thank You. Amen."

"God my Father, calm my spirit and direct my path."

"God, I have made mistakes. I am sorry. I am Your child, though, and seek to be united to You."

"I believe in God. I believe Jesus is calling me. I believe my Blessed Mother has requested my help. Therefore I am going to pray on this day and every day."

"God my Father, help me to understand."

Prayers to Jesus

"Jesus, I give You my day."

"Jesus, how do You want to use me on this day? You have a willing servant in me, Jesus. Allow me to work for the Kingdom."

"Lord, what can I do today to prepare for Your coming? Direct me, Lord, and I will see to Your wishes."

"Lord, help me."

"Jesus, love me."

Prayers to the Angels

"Angels from Heaven, direct my path."

"Dearest angel guardian, I desire to serve Jesus by remaining at peace. Please obtain for me the graces necessary to maintain His divine peace in my heart."

Prayers for a Struggling Soul

"Jesus, what do You think of all this? Jesus, what do You want me to do for this soul? Jesus, show me how to bring You into this situation."

"Angel guardian, thank you for your constant vigil over this soul. Saints in Heaven, please assist this dear angel."

Prayers for Children

"God in Heaven, You are the Creator of all things. Please send Your graces down upon our world."

"Jesus, I love You."

"Jesus, I trust in You. Jesus, I trust in You. Jesus, I trust in You."

"Jesus, I offer You my day."

"Mother Mary, help me to be good."

How to Pray the Rosary

1. Make the Sign of the Cross and say the "Apostles Creed."
2. Say the "Our Father."
3. Say three "Hail Marys."
4. Say the "Glory be to the Father."
5. Announce the First Mystery; then say the "Our Father."
6. Say ten "Hail Marys," while meditating on the Mystery.
7. Say the "Glory be to the Father." After each decade say the following prayer requested by the Blessed Virgin Mary at Fatima: "O my Jesus, forgive us our sins, save us from the fires of hell, lead all souls to Heaven, especially those in most need of Thy mercy."
8. Announce the Second Mystery: then say the "Our Father." Repeat 6 and 7 and continue with the Third, Fourth, and Fifth Mysteries in the same manner.
9. Say the "Hail, Holy Queen" on the medal after the five decades are completed.

As a general rule, depending on the season, the Joyful Mysteries are said on Monday and Saturday; the Sorrowful Mysteries on Tuesday and Friday;

the Glorious Mysteries on Wednesday and Sunday; and the Luminous Mysteries on Thursday.

Papal Reflections of the Mysteries

The Joyful Mysteries

The Joyful Mysteries are marked by the joy radiating from the event of the Incarnation. This is clear from the very first mystery, the Annunciation, where Gabriel's greeting to the Virgin of Nazareth is linked to an invitation to messianic joy: "Rejoice, Mary." The whole of salvation... had led up to this greeting. (Prayed on Mondays and Saturdays, and optional on Sundays during Advent and the Christmas Season.)

The Luminous Mysteries

Moving on from the infancy and the hidden life in Nazareth to the public life of Jesus, our contemplation brings us to those mysteries which may be called in a special way "Mysteries of Light." Certainly, the whole mystery of Christ is a mystery of light. He is the "Light of the world" (John 8:12). Yet this truth emerges in a special way during the years of His public life. (Prayed on Thursdays.)

The Sorrowful Mysteries

The Gospels give great prominence to the Sorrowful Mysteries of Christ. From the beginning, Christian piety, especially during the Lenten devotion of the Way of the Cross, has focused on the individual moments of the Passion, realizing that here is found the culmination of the revelation of God's love and the source of our salvation. (Prayed on Tuesdays and Fridays, and optional on Sundays during Lent.)

The Glorious Mysteries

"The contemplation of Christ's face cannot stop at the image of the Crucified One. He is the Risen One!" The Rosary has always expressed this knowledge born of faith and invited the believer to pass beyond the darkness of the Passion in order to gaze upon Christ's glory in the Resurrection and Ascension… Mary herself would be raised to that same glory in the Assumption. (Prayed on Wednesdays and Sundays.)

From the *Apostolic Letter The Rosary of the Virgin Mary*, Pope John Paul II, Oct. 16, 2002.

Prayers of the Rosary

The Sign of the Cross

In the name of the Father, and of the Son, and of the Holy Spirit. Amen.

The Apostles' Creed

I believe in God, the Father Almighty, Creator of Heaven and earth. I believe in Jesus Christ, His only Son, our Lord. He was conceived by the power of the Holy Spirit and born of the Virgin Mary. He suffered under Pontius Pilate, was crucified, died, and was buried. He descended into hell. On the third day He rose again from the dead. He ascended into Heaven, and is seated at the right hand of the Father. He will come again to judge the living and the dead. I believe in the Holy Spirit, the holy Catholic Church, the Communion of Saints, the forgiveness of sins, the resurrection of the body, and life everlasting. Amen.

Our Father

Our Father, who art in Heaven, hallowed be Thy name. Thy Kingdom come. Thy will be done on earth as it is in Heaven. Give us this day our daily bread. And forgive us our trespasses, as we forgive those who trespass against us. And lead us not into temptation, but deliver us from evil. Amen.

Hail Mary

Hail Mary, full of grace, the Lord is with thee. Blessed art thou among women, and blessed is the fruit of thy womb, Jesus. Holy Mary, Mother of God, pray for us sinners, now and at the hour of our death. Amen.

Glory Be to the Father

Glory be to the Father, and to the Son, and to the Holy Spirit. As it was in the beginning, is now, and ever shall be, world without end. Amen.

Hail Holy Queen

Hail, Holy Queen, Mother of Mercy, our life, our sweetness and our hope. To thee do we cry, poor banished children of Eve. To thee do we send up our sighs, mourning and weeping in this valley of tears. Turn then, most gracious Advocate, thine eyes of mercy towards us. And after this, our exile, show unto us the blessed fruit of thy womb, Jesus. O clement, O loving, O sweet Virgin Mary!

Pray for us, O Holy Mother of God.
That we may be made worthy of the promises of Christ.

The Mysteries

First Joyful Mystery:
The Annunciation

And when the angel had come to her, he said, "Hail, full of grace, the Lord is with thee. Blessed art thou among women." *(Luke* 1:28)

One *Our Father*, Ten *Hail Marys*,
One *Glory Be*, etc.

Fruit of the Mystery: ***Humility***

Second Joyful Mystery:
The Visitation

Elizabeth was filled with the Holy Spirit and cried out in a loud voice: "Blest are you among women and blest is the fruit of your womb."*(Luke* 1:41-42)

One *Our Father*, Ten *Hail Marys*,
One *Glory Be*, etc.

Fruit of the Mystery: ***Love of Neighbor***

Third Joyful Mystery:
The Birth of Jesus

She gave birth to her first-born Son and wrapped Him in swaddling clothes and laid Him in a manger, because there was no room for them in the place where travelers lodged. *(Luke* 2:7)

One *Our Father*, Ten *Hail Marys*,
One *Glory Be*, etc.

Fruit of the Mystery: ***Poverty***

Fourth Joyful Mystery:
The Presentation

When the day came to purify them according to the law of Moses, the couple brought Him up to Jerusalem so that He could be presented to the Lord, for it is written in the law of the Lord, "Every first-born male shall be consecrated to the Lord."

(Luke 2:22-23)

One *Our Father*, Ten *Hail Marys*,
One *Glory Be*, etc.

Fruit of the Mystery: ***Obedience***

Fifth Joyful Mystery:
The Finding of the Child Jesus in the Temple

On the third day they came upon Him in the temple sitting in the midst of the teachers, listening to them and asking them questions. *(Luke* 2:46)

One *Our Father*, Ten *Hail Marys*,
One *Glory Be*, etc.

Fruit of the Mystery: ***Joy in Finding Jesus***

First Luminous Mystery:
The Baptism of Jesus

And when Jesus was baptized... the heavens were opened and He saw the Spirit of God descending like a dove, and alighting on Him, and lo, a voice from heaven, saying "this is My beloved Son," with whom I am well pleased." *(Matthew* 3:16-17)

One *Our Father*, Ten *Hail Marys*,
One *Glory Be*, etc.

Fruit of the Mystery: ***Openness to the Holy Spirit***

Second Luminous Mystery:
The Wedding at Cana

His mother said to the servants, "Do whatever He tells you."… Jesus said to them, "Fill the jars with water." And they filled them up to the brim.

(John 2:5-7)

One Our Father, Ten Hail Marys,
One Glory Be, etc.

Fruit of the Mystery: ***To Jesus through Mary***

Third Luminous Mystery:
The Proclamation of the Kingdom of God

"And preach as you go, saying, 'The kingdom of heaven is at hand.' Heal the sick, raise the dead, cleanse lepers, cast out demons. You received without pay, give without pay." (*Matthew* 10:7-8)

One Our Father, Ten Hail Marys,
One Glory Be, etc.

Fruit of the Mystery: ***Repentance and Trust in God***

Fourth Luminous Mystery:
The Transfiguration

And as He was praying, the appearance of His countenance was altered and His raiment become dazzling white. And a voice came out of the cloud saying, "This is My Son, My chosen; listen to Him!

(Luke 9:29, 35)

One Our Father, Ten Hail Marys,
One Glory Be, etc.

Fruit of the Mystery: ***Desire for Holiness***

Fifth Luminous Mystery:
The Institution of the Eucharist

And He took bread, and when He had given thanks He broke it and gave it to them, saying, "This is My body which is given for you."… And likewise the cup after supper, saying, "This cup which is poured out for you is the new covenant in My blood."

(Luke 22:19-20)

One Our Father, Ten Hail Marys,
One Glory Be, etc.

Fruit of the Mystery: ***Adoration***

First Sorrowful Mystery:
The Agony in the Garden

In His anguish He prayed with all the greater intensity, and His sweat became like drops of blood falling to the ground. Then He rose from prayer and came to His disciples, only to find them asleep, exhausted with grief.   (*Luke* 22:44-45)

One Our Father, Ten Hail Marys,
One Glory Be, etc.

Fruit of the Mystery: ***Sorrow for Sin***

Second Sorrowful Mystery:
The Scourging at the Pillar

Pilate's next move was to take Jesus and have Him scourged.   (*John* 19:1)

One Our Father, Ten Hail Marys,
One Glory Be, etc.

Fruit of the Mystery: ***Purity***

Third Sorrowful Mystery:
The Crowning with Thorns

They stripped off His clothes and wrapped Him in a scarlet military cloak. Weaving a crown out of thorns they fixed it on His head, and stuck a reed in His right hand...   (*Matthew* 27:28-29)

One *Our Father*, Ten *Hail Marys*,
One *Glory Be*, etc.

Fruit of the Mystery: ***Courage***

Fourth Sorrowful Mystery:
The Carrying of the Cross

... carrying the cross by Himself, He went out to what is called the Place of the Skull (in Hebrew, Golgotha).   (*John* 19:17)

One *Our Father*, Ten *Hail Marys*,
One *Glory Be*, etc.

Fruit of the Mystery: ***Patience***

Fifth Sorrowful Mystery:
The Crucifixion

Jesus uttered a loud cry and said, "Father, into Your hands I commend My spirit." After He said this, He expired.   (*Luke* 23:46)

One *Our Father*, Ten *Hail Marys*,
One *Glory Be*, etc.

Fruit of the Mystery: ***Perseverance***

First Glorious Mystery:
The Resurrection

You need not be amazed! You are looking for Jesus of Nazareth, the one who was crucified. He has been raised up; He is not here. See the place where they laid Him." *(Mark* 16:6)

One *Our Father*, Ten *Hail Marys*,
One *Glory Be*, etc.

Fruit of the Mystery: **Faith**

Second Glorious Mystery:
The Ascension

Then, after speaking to them, the Lord Jesus was taken up into Heaven and took His seat at God's right hand. *(Mark* 16:19)

One *Our Father*, Ten *Hail Marys*,
One *Glory Be*, etc.

Fruit of the Mystery: **Hope**

Third Glorious Mystery:
The Descent of the Holy Spirit

All were filled with the Holy Spirit. They began to express themselves in foreign tongues and make bold proclamation as the Spirit prompted them.

(Acts 2:4)

One *Our Father*, Ten *Hail Marys*,
One *Glory Be*, etc.

Fruit of the Mystery: **Love of God**

Fourth Glorious Mystery:
The Assumption

You are the glory of Jerusalem... you are the splendid boast of our people... God is pleased with what you have wrought. May you be blessed by the Lord Almighty forever and ever.

(*Judith* 15:9-10)

One *Our Father*, Ten *Hail Marys*,
One *Glory Be*, etc.

Fruit of the Mystery: ***Grace of a Happy Death***

Fifth Glorious Mystery:
The Coronation

A great sign appeared in the sky, a woman clothed with the sun, with the moon under her feet, and on her head a crown of twelve stars. (*Revelation* 12:1)

One *Our Father*, Ten *Hail Marys*,
One *Glory Be*, etc.

Fruit of the Mystery: ***Trust in Mary's Intercession***

How to Pray the Chaplet of Divine Mercy

The Chaplet of Divine Mercy is a prayer which Jesus taught St. Faustina Kowalska. The chaplet offers us a special means to pray for mercy for ourselves and the whole world.

The Chaplet of Mercy is recited using ordinary rosary beads of five decades. The chaplet is preceded by two opening prayers from the *Diary* of Saint Faustina and followed by a closing prayer.

1. Make the Sign of the Cross

2. Say the Two Opening Prayers

"You expired, Jesus, but the source of life gushed forth for souls, and the ocean of mercy opened up for the whole world. O Fount of Life, unfathomable Divine Mercy, envelop the whole world and empty Yourself out upon us."

"O Blood and Water, which gushed forth from the Heart of Jesus as a fountain of mercy for us, I trust in You!"

3. Say the Our Father

4. Say the Hail Mary

5. Say the Apostles' Creed

6. On each large bead pray the Eternal Father Prayer:

"Eternal Father, I offer You the Body and Blood, Soul and Divinity of Your dearly beloved Son, our Lord, Jesus Christ, in atonement for our sins and those of the whole world."

7. On each of the ten small beads of the decade pray:

"For the sake of His Sorrowful Passion, have mercy on us and on the whole world."

8. Repeat prayers 6 and 7 for the remaining decades

Concluding Prayers

9. Say the Holy God prayer

"Holy God, Holy Mighty One, Holy Immortal One, have mercy on us and on the whole world."

10. Optional Closing Prayer

"Eternal God, in whom mercy is endless and the treasury of compassion inexhaustible, look kindly upon us and increase Your mercy in us, that in difficult moments we might not despair nor become despondent, but with great confidence submit ourselves to Your holy will, which is Love and Mercy itself."

To learn more about the image of The Divine Mercy, the Chaplet of Divine Mercy and the series of revelations given to St. Faustina Kowalska please contact:

Marians of the Immaculate Conception
Stockbridge, Massachusetts 01263
Telephone 800-462-7426
www.marian.org

Appendix

The Volumes

Direction for Our Times
as given to Anne, a lay apostle

Volume One:	***Thoughts on Spirituality***
Volume Two:	***Conversations with the Eucharistic Heart of Jesus***
Volume Three:	***God the Father Speaks to His Children*** ***The Blessed Mother Speaks to Her Bishops and Priests***
Volume Four:	***Jesus the King*** ***Heaven Speaks to Priests*** ***Jesus Speaks to Sinners***
Volume Five:	***Jesus the Redeemer***
Volume Six:	***Heaven Speaks to Families***
Volume Seven:	***Greetings from Heaven***
Volume Eight:	***Resting in the Heart of the Savior***
Volume Nine:	***Angels***
Volume Ten:	***Jesus Speaks to His Apostles***

The Volumes are now available in PDF format for
free download and printing from our website:
<u>www.directionforourtimes.org</u>.
We encourage everyone to print and distribute them.

The Volumes are also available at your local bookstore.

The "Heaven Speaks" Booklets

*Direction for Our Times
as given to Anne, a lay apostle*

The following booklets are available individually from Direction for Our Times:

Heaven Speaks About Abortion
Heaven Speaks About Addictions
Heaven Speaks to Victims of Clerical Abuse
Heaven Speaks to Consecrated Souls
Heaven Speaks About Depression
Heaven Speaks About Divorce
Heaven Speaks to Prisoners
Heaven Speaks to Soldiers
Heaven Speaks About Stress
Heaven Speaks to Young Adults

Heaven Speaks to Those Away from the Church
Heaven Speaks to Those Considering Suicide
Heaven Speaks to Those Who Do Not Know Jesus
Heaven Speaks to Those Who Are Dying
Heaven Speaks to Those Who Experience Tragedy
Heaven Speaks to Those Who Fear Purgatory
Heaven Speaks to Those Who Have Rejected God
Heaven Speaks to Those Who Struggle to Forgive
**Heaven Speaks to Those Who Suffer from
 Financial Need**
**Heaven Speaks to Parents Who Worry About
 Their Children's Salvation**

All twenty of the "Heaven Speaks" booklets are now available in PDF format for free download and printing from our website www.directionforourtimes.org. We encourage everyone to print and distribute these booklets.

Appendix

Other books by Anne, a lay apostle

Climbing the Mountain
Discovering your path to holiness
Anne's experiences of Heaven

The Mist of Mercy
Spiritual Warfare
Anne's experiences of Purgatory

Serving In Clarity
A Guide for Lay Apostles
of Jesus Christ the Returning King

In Defense of Obedience
and
Reflections on the Priesthood
Two Essays on topics close to the Heart of Jesus

Lessons in Love
Moving Toward Divine Intimacy

Whispers from the Cross
Reclaiming the Church
Through Personal Holiness

This book is part of a non-profit mission. Our Lord has requested that we spread these words internationally. Please help us.

In Ireland:
Direction For Our Times
The Hague Building
Cullies
Cavan
County Cavan

+353-(0)49-437-3040
contactus@dfot.ie

Registered Charity CHY17298

In the USA:
Direction For Our Times
9000 West 81st Street
Justice, Illinois 60458

708-496-9300
contactus@directionfor
ourtimes.org

A 501(c)(3) Organization

Adult Faith Formation

We are currently offering Adult Faith Formation programs. Please check our website for our most recent events including weekend retreats and our annual School of Holiness held each summer in Ireland. To learn more about these programs please contact one of our offices.